STILL FIRETALKING

by

Patricia Polacco

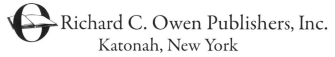
Richard C. Owen Publishers, Inc.
Katonah, New York

Meet the Author

Text copyright © 2014 by Patricia Polacco

Library of Congress Cataloging-in-Publication Data

Library of Congress Control Number: 2013922307
978-1-57274-990-0 paperback
978-1-57274-992-4 hardcover

Richard C. Owen Publishers, Inc.
PO Box 585
Katonah, New York 10536

The text type was set in Garamond Premier Pro
Design/production credit:
    Douglas Abdelnour Bedford Photo-Graphic, Inc., Somers, New York
    Ginny Tormey Digital Arts Professional, Katonah, New York

Printed in Canada
10 9 8 7 6

For more information about our collection of Meet the Author books and other children's books, visit our website at www.RCOwen.com or call 1-800-336-5588.

To my family

I was born on July 11, 1944, in Lansing, Michigan,
and grew up in Union City until my parents divorced.
Then my mother, my brother Richard, and I moved
to Oakland, California. Every summer, though,
Richard and I went back to Michigan to live with our dad.

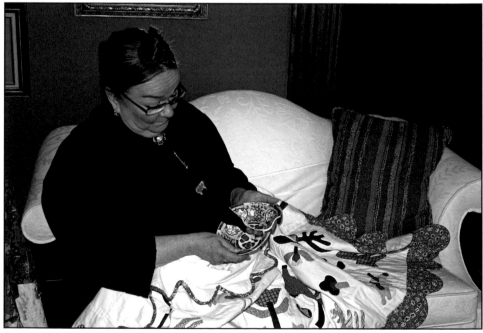

My mother's people were Russian and my father's people were Irish. In *The Keeping Quilt* and *The Blessing Cup*, I tell how my mother's family came to be in America. The cup was broken during an earthquake in California. The original quilt now

hangs in the Mazza Museum at the University of Findlay

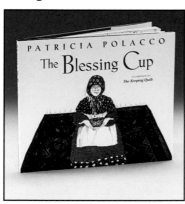

in Findlay, Ohio. My beloved sister-in-law and her quilting guild made me an exact replica that we now take to school visits, wedding chuppas, to celebrate new babies, to use as a tablecloth, and for other special occasions.

Fiona's Lace tells the story of how my father's family came from Ireland. Both sets of my grandparents were amazing storytellers. With almost no urging at all they squinted up their eyes, watched our faces, and began to "tell."

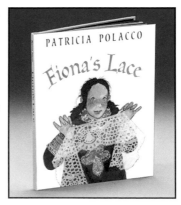

Many of our evenings were spent in front of the fireplace, popping corn, eating apple wedges, and hearing rich, incredible tales. My babushka (my Ukrainian grandmother) called this "firetalking." Whenever she finished one of her tales of magic and mystery, my brother and I would always ask, "Bubby, is that a true story?" She would look at us and reply, "Of course it's true... but it might not have happened."

It was she who taught me to make beautiful, decorated, *Pysanky* eggs. Because I have such a special love for these Ukrainian eggs, I wrote a story about them called *Rechenka's Eggs.*

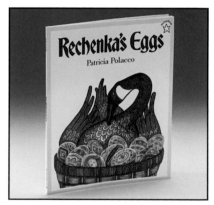

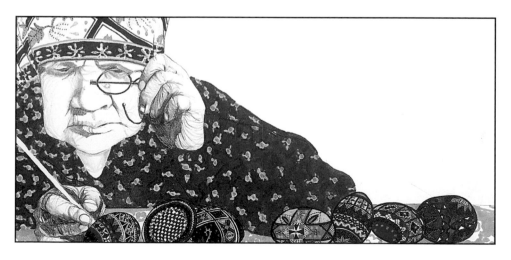

9

My summers with my dad are golden memories. He was a traveling salesman and was on the road a lot. But when Richard and I were with him, he took time off to be with us. We went fishing, took long walks in the woods, and spent almost every other waking hour on horseback. He raised horses and took delight in teaching me their secrets and noble ways.

Our school year was spent in Oakland with my mom.
Her house was always filled with beautiful music and
lovely things to look at and touch.

She saw to it that I took ballet and studied art and
drama. I loved it when she framed my drawings and
hung them up in the house.

In both Mom's house and at Dad's place there was always a rocking chair, just for me. I spent hours and hours just rocking and dreaming every day. I spent a lot of time in my imagination. It soothed the pain of not doing well in school.

I had difficulty reading. Math was and still is almost impossible for me. I knew that inside I was very smart, but at school I felt stupid and slow. I had to work very hard to learn things. Now that I am grown up I realize that I process information differently than most people do. My brain scrambles images that my eyes see.

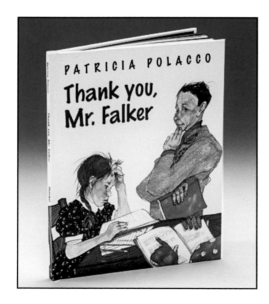

Once I got the hang of it, I went on in school. I even ended up graduating from college, and getting my Ph.D. in Art History. My experiences learning to read and write prompted me to write *Thank You, Mr. Falker.*

I didn't start writing and illustrating children's books until I was 41 years old! Before that I was busy being a mother and working for museums restoring ancient icons. I have two children, a daughter and a son. They are grown now.

After living in Oakland, California for almost 41 years, I longed to return to Michigan. In 1994 I bought a beautiful old mansion that was built before the Civil War.

Abraham Lincoln actually walked through my house when it was a stage stop. He was running for president and had just given a speech in Jackson, Michigan. He was on his way to the rail station in Kalamazoo to return to his home in Springfield, Illinois.

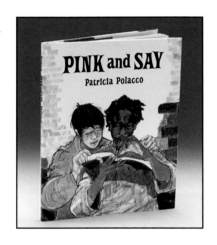

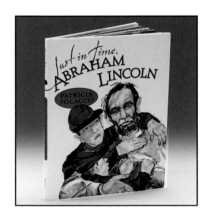

I have written two books that feature President Lincoln: *Pink and Say* and *Just in Time, Abraham Lincoln.* My great, great grandfather fought in the civil war and shook Mr. Lincoln's hand at Bull Run.

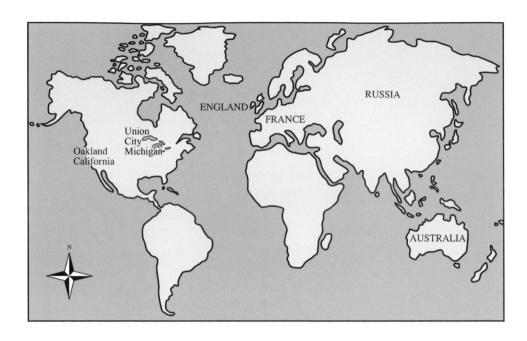

I have lived and studied in Australia, England, France and Russia, Oakland and Berkeley. I now live in Union City, Michigan.

My lovely home, besides being my residence, is also a rescue farm for unwanted, sick, and injured animals. I have goats, sheep, horses, dogs, and many, many cats.

One of my favorite books when I was a little girl was *Millions of Cats* by Wanda Gag. Cats and goats are in just about all of my books. Two of my books about cats are *Mrs. Katz and Tush* and *For the Love of Autumn.*

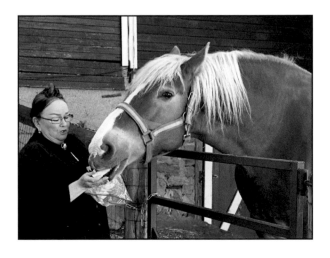

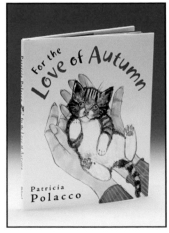

Since moving to Union City, I have devoted my life not only to animals but also the children of this village. I bought an old Victorian firehouse and renovated it.

The firehouse is now a center for art, music, and drama. We put on performances, concerts, holiday events, and programs for children. Every Christmas Santa actually comes here and brings a reindeer or two!

A few years ago I bought an old farmhouse and turned it into one of the most popular haunted houses in five counties. I wrote the book *The Graves Family* to convince the people in town that they actually lived there.

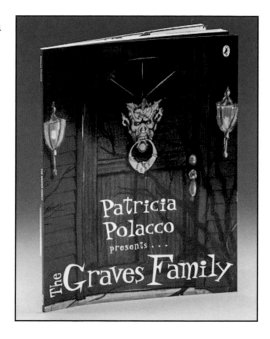

On Halloween night almost 3000 children and their families come through the Graves House. I become Mrs. Graves.

My son,
Steven, is a
tenured
university
professor
and teaches
art and art
history.

My daughter, Traci,
has a degree in
psychology, personal
communication, and
medicine. Both of my
children and other
family members
appear in many of
my books.

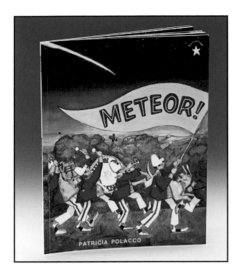

Before my mother's death in 1996, she was an avid collector of geodes and rocks, probably because they reminded her of the meteor that she saw crash into her yard when she was a little girl. I wrote *Meteor!*, my first book, to share that incredible event with all of you.

The big one that landed in my mother's yard is now our family headstone in Riverside Cemetery, less than two blocks from my farm. In our family we believe that if we touch it and make wishes on it, the wishes come true. I take a piece of that meteor to schools with me and invite kids to wish on it!

As a matter of fact our village celebrates that meteor every summer at The Meteor Festival. Teachers, librarians,

and children from all over the country attend. It is a celebration of literature, art, drama, and music. We have guest authors, concerts, plays, horse-drawn buggy rides, house and studio tours, and sometimes a bonfire.

During the winter we host a holiday event. I display over 22 trees in my home and studio. We raise money for our food pantry and local charities. My concerns about the welfare of children have influenced me in topics I write about, including *Bully*, a recent favorite of mine.

I am lucky... so very lucky! I love my life. Can you imagine
doing what you love every day? When I am working on a
book, I work every day until it is finished. The first thing
I do in the morning, though, just like I did when I was a
little girl, is sit and rock. I listen to music and let my
imagination soar. I take rocking so seriously I have at least
one or two rockers in every room in my house!

When I rock, my thoughts boil
in my head. They catch the
air and fly. The images
and stories come with
fury and energy. I feel
like Appelemando in
Appelemando's Dreams.
My stories float above me!

I jot down thoughts and
outlines, capturing ideas
before they disappear.
Many of the stories are
rooted in my own childhood
memories of people and
events important to me.

After I have fed all my animals and finished with morning chores my day usually begins with writing. I do not use a computer. I use an electric typewriter.

I take the hundreds of little notes I made while rocking and begin to type my story as if I am describing to all of you a movie that I have just seen.

My manuscripts are usually only 8 pages long. But then I send them along to my editor who is just like your teacher. She will read the manuscript and make "corrections." Marks appear all over my paper.

Then I rewrite and rewrite and rewrite! I fix story parts that don't work. I condense writing that is too long. I expand story ideas that need more detail. I look for better words and better ways to tell my story.

My heart sings whenever I am drawing. As far back as I can remember, I knew that drawing connected me somehow to the universe and maybe even to God.

When I do illustrations for a book, I first draw everything in pencil. I make what is called a "rough dummy." It looks exactly like the finished book, except it's in black and white.

I use those drawings to make the "color finishes." I draw the layout in pencil, then I "lay in" the color with markers, acrylic paint, oil paint, pastels, and inks.

Sometimes I cut out photographs of real people and paste them into my artwork. I can't tell you how many times I have made my family, my friends, and even my neighbors stop what they were doing to pose for me. I don't always  get my drawings right the first time!

Sometimes, as with my stories, I have to do them over and over again.

Some days I go to schools and give author programs. Sometimes I fly to other cities to talk to children, teachers, and librarians. This year I made a special trip to California to be present at the birth of my first grandchild. His name is Enzo and we have already started telling him stories. One day he will join us in front of the fireplace to hear a glorious tale told from the heart. After the "firetalking," he will be sure to ask, "Bubby, is that a true story?" The answer is, "Of course it's true. . . but it might not have happened."

Other books by Patricia Polacco

Patricia Polacco has now written and illustrated about 90 titles! Here is a sampling you will find in bookstores and libraries.

Rechenka's Eggs; The Junkyard Wonders; The Keeping Quilt (25th Anniversary Edition); Thank You, Mr. Falker; Pink and Say; The Blessing Cup; Ginger and Petunia; Clara and Davie; Mrs. Katz and Tush; Mr. Wayne's Masterpiece; The Art of Miss Chew; For the Love of Autumn; All Because of Thursday; Gifts of the Heart

Acknowledgements

Photograph of Patricia Polacco on cover of *Still Firetalking* copyright © 2013 by Traci Polacco. Photograph on title page, pages 6 bottom, 9 top, 15, 16, 17, 18, 19, 23, 24, 26, 27, 28, and 29 copyright © 2013 by Raymond and Elizabeth Westra. Photographs on page 6 top and 31 copyright © 2013 by Christina Hernandez. Photographs on pages 14, 21, and 22 copyright © 1994 by Lawrence Migdale. Photographs on pages 4 ,10, 11, 12, 13, and 20 appear courtesy of Patricia Polacco. Cover photographs for the following books written and illustrated by Patricia Polacco included by permission of Simon &Schuster Books for Young Readers, a trademark of Simon & Schuster: *The Keeping Quilt, The Blessing Cup, Fiona's Lace.* Illustration on page 8 from *My Rotten Red Headed Older Brother* copyright © 1994 by Patricia Polacco used by arrangement with Simon & Schuster Books for Young Readers, a trademark of Simon & Schuster. Cover photographs for the following books written and illustrated by Patricia Polacco included by permission of Penguin Group (USA) LLC All rights reserved: *Rechenka's Eggs; Thank You, Mr. Falker; Pink and Say; Just in Time, Abraham Lincoln; For the Love of Autumn; The Graves Family; Meteor!; Bully; Appelemando's Dreams.* Illustration on page 9 from *Rechenka's Eggs*, copyright © 1988 by Patricia Polacco included by permission of Penguin Group (USA) LLC All rights reserved. Illustration on page 25 from *Appelemando's Dreams*, copyright © 1991 by Patricia Polacco included by permission of Penguin Group (USA) LLC All rights reserved. Cover photograph for the following book written and illustrated by Patricia Polacco included by permission of Random House Children's Books: *Mrs. Katz and Tush.*